Chasing our Roots
......and then some

Joanne Simon Tailele & Richard Alan Simon

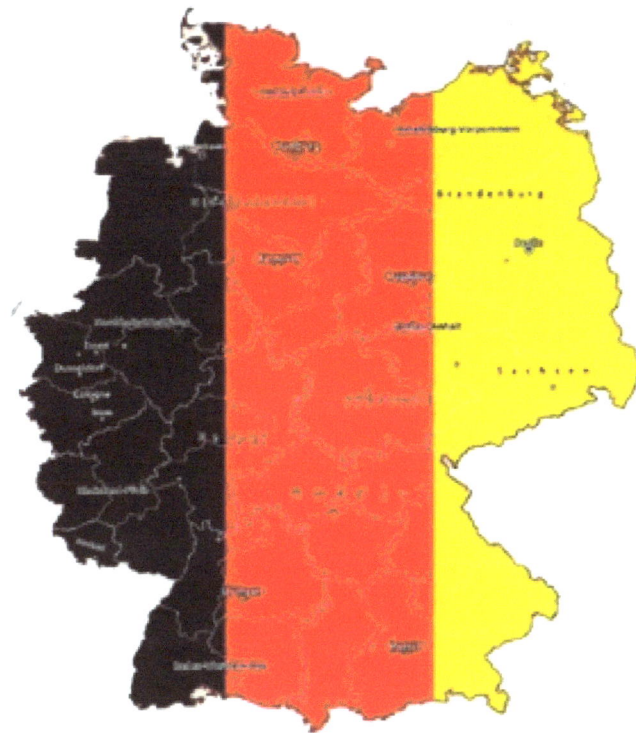

ISBN-13: 978-0-692-15702-2

Europe Trip   May 18-June 3, 2018

Written by Joanne, additional notes by Dick

Friday, May 18, 2018 - Dick arrived at Steve's in Las Vegas with Willis, his dashshund.

Saturday, May 19, 2018 - Dick showed Steve how to administer Willis' insulin and test glucose.
Joanne arrived at Terri's in Miami to leave her car and stay the night.

Sunday, May 20, 2018 - Dick's flight left Las Vegas 8:30 a.m., connecting through Houston and was due to arrive Fort Lauderdale on United #1899 at 8:11 p.m. His flight from Houston was delayed so he was too late to have dinner at the airport with Terri as planned. He ended up at the far end of the terminal from international flights. It took awhile to find the right gate and Joanne. Terri drove Joanne to airport and they had dinner together. We left Fort Lauderdale on Norwegian Airlines Flight DY7042 to Copenhagen, Denmark at 24:45 (12:45 p.m.) about an hour late.

The nine-hour flight to Copenhagen was easy. We both slept off and on. I was glad I had Terri's neck pillow. It helped a lot.
Dick had one too, but it was smaller and not as effective.

Denmark

Sweden

Germany

Austria

Monday May 21, 2018 –

Copenhagen, Denmark

Arriving in Copenhagen at 14:45 (2:45 p.m.), we took the train from the airport to the main train terminal in Copenhagen. Stopped at a juice bar for a drink. Dick bought us each a Copenhagen City Pass that gave us entry into most attractions including bus and train rides within the city and to Helsingör. Looking over the map, we realized we were only about eight blocks from the hotel, so we decided to walk. Not bad with roller bags and backpacks.

We checked in the Danshotel City Center. Quiet at check-in. We had a nice view from our room of the Indehavren River, but no balcony. The room had a bunk beds and two single beds. Dick took the bottom bunk and I took one of the singles. Room was clean but very sparse. At least it had its own bathroom with a shower.

We walked over the Langebro Bridge right next to the hostel that goes over the inner harbor connecting the city with Christianshavn. We had dinner at an Italian restaurant called Ponte Vecchio. Later, we walked over to Tivoli Garden (included on the Copenhagen City Pass). It was closing up so very little was open but it was pretty with the lights on.

Copenhagen Train Station

Tivoli Gardens

Danshotel, Copenhagen

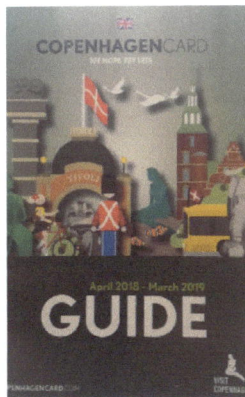

Langebro Bridge, Copenhagen, Denmark

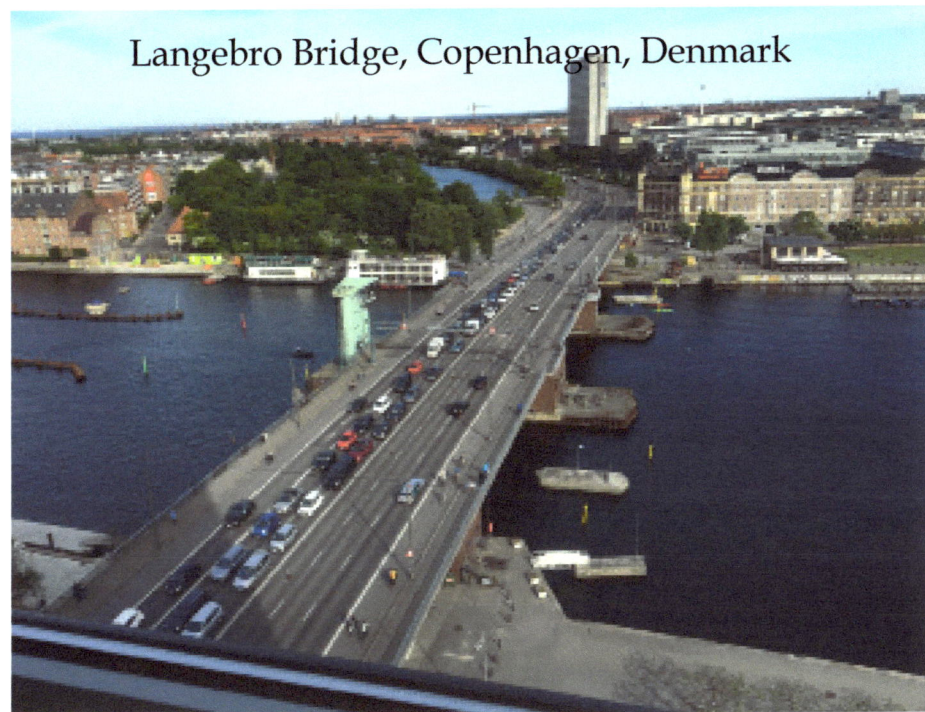

Tuesday, May 22, 2018

It started to get light about 4 a.m. I wasn't feeling any jet lag as I expected. We had breakfast at the hotel, typical Scandinavian breakfast of open face sandwich, rather dry brown bread with thin slices of cheeses, meats like ham and pork. (Discovered that it is customary for most hotels to include these breakfasts.)

We spend the day in Copenhagen. Very impressed with all the cyclists and the great bike paths. Hundreds of people of all ages bike back and forth to work as evidenced by the amount of bicycle traffic and the huge bike parking available everywhere. My guess would be that at least 50% or more Danes use bicycles as their main source of transportation in Copenhagen.

I wanted to see the Hans Christian Anderson Museum. It was small and hard to find since we were expecting something much larger. It was wedged in a narrow space next to the Ripley's Believe it or Not. The museum walked us through the famous children's author's many stories that he created with places to stop and listen to the stories with a choice of language in front of still mannequins.. I was disappointed there was nowhere to buy any Hans Christian Anderson books. Dick took my picture standing on the statue of H.C. Anderson outside of City Hall.

We walked to the National Museum It was very modern with several mezanines that looked down on to the main level. Each room was a different era, dating back to the pre-historic times, Viking times and progressing to the current day.

Dick bought our lunch in the restaurant at the museum. I had an open-face chicken salad sandwich. What is with all this open-face stuff? Not my favorite way to eat. A traditional Danish open-faced sandwich consists of a small slice of hard grainy bread that is fried then topped with either cold meats, fish, cheese, and fresh vegetable or spouts combinations. They are similar to tapas but a little larger. That day the waiter was suggesting three sandwiches per person, but we each only had one. Dick's sandwich was steak tar-tar (raw beef). He was expecting it to be thinly sliced but it was marinated ground beef and topped with some sprouts which naturally he didn't eat. He said it was good but way too much beef.

At the gift shop on the main level, I found a Hans Christian Anderson book in English with all of his famous stories, including my favorites, *The Little Mermaid* and *The Little Match Girl.* Dick bought a gift/souvenir as well.

Christiansborg Palace, Copenhagen

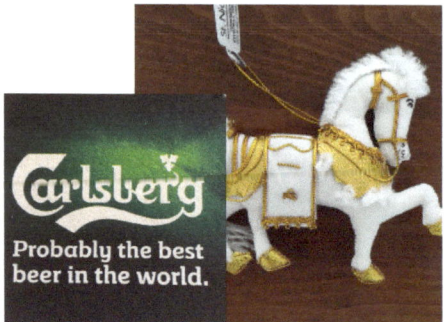

Carlsberg
Probably the best
beer in the world.

Next stop was the Christiansborg Palace. From the tower (*which had an elevator*), we had a wonderful 360°view of the whole city. They told us that the Queen and her family did not live there anymore but lived very close by in Amalienborg. Today it houses the working offices of the Royal Family and the offices of the Danish prime minister and Danish parliament. We visited the Royal Stables, built in 1745 where they house the white horses, 14-16 present day, but at one time held as many 250 horses. We saw the Royal carriages, some that are still in use today. It was the only part of the 1731 Castle that was not destroyed in the 1794 fire. Preparations were in play for the celebration of the Prince's 50th birthday party in two days. We could not see the Great Room because of the preparations for the birthday celebration but we did go into the Royal Kitchen. They said that much of the food is actually prepared at Amalienborg now and brought over just before serving.

Under the Palace, we could see the ruins of the previous versions of the Castle. The first castle was built in 1167 and was destroyed by fire in 1629. It was rebuilt in 1638; demolished in 1731 to build the 3rd castle. But the 1794 fire destroyed most of it and what we see today was rebuilt in 1928.

We took a canal tour which showed us many of the sites of Copenhagen we never would have seen by foot. The tour guide did a terrific job and explained everything in four languages. One of the sites was the The Little Mermaid statue built after the Hans Christian Anderson fairytale. It was much smaller than I expected, and since it faced inland, we only saw the back of her. We went under dozens of low bridges, so low that everyone had to stay seated not to hit their heads on the underside of the bridges. Some very quaint neighborhoods that lined the canal were very inviting with colorful homes, boats anchored in the canals, rows of house-boats moored together.

We had dinner at Strickers in Copenhagen. We both had Fish and Chips and beer. I discovered I really liked Carlsberg beer. Lots of teenagers checked in to the hostel that day as a large group. Kids being kids, they ran up and down hallways and were not very quiet until late at night.

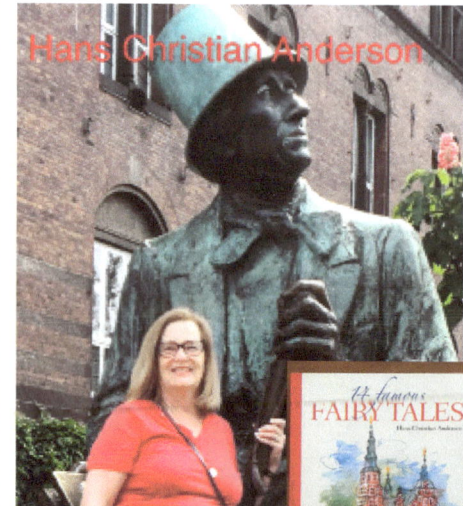

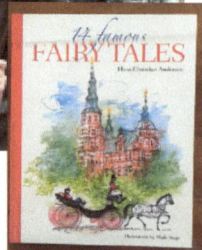

Hans Christian Anderson

FAIRY TALES

Christiansborg Palace

Copenhagen canal ride

The Little Mermaid

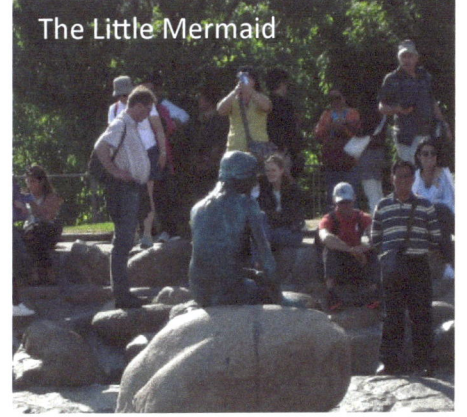

Copenhagen, Denmark

Kronborg

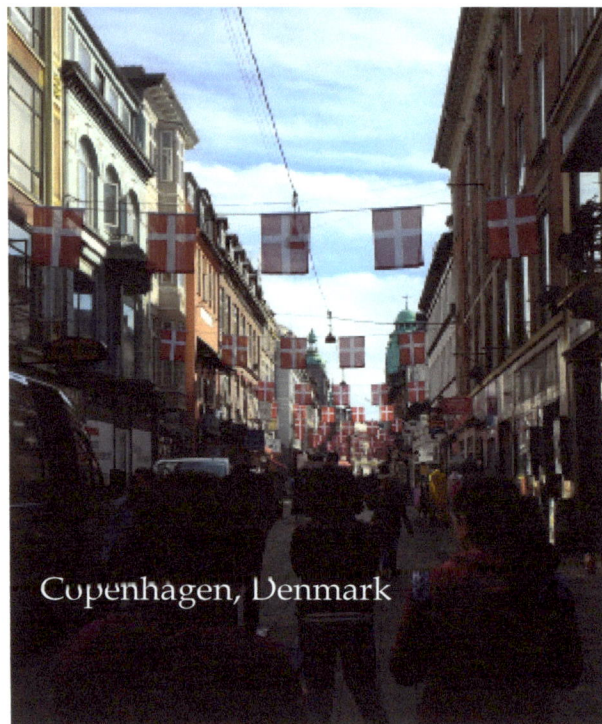
Copenhagen, Denmark

Wednesday, May 23, 2018

Helsingor, Denmark

After breakfast at the hostel with tons of kids around, we checked out and took a cab to the train station. The cabby was grumpy because it was such a short fare. We were going to Uber but the front desk clerk told us that they banned Uber since it took too much business away from the cabs.

We took the train to Helsingör, Denmark. We left our luggage at the 7/11 at the train station for 50 Danish krona each ($7.83 US). We laughed at how strange this seemed, but the gentleman gladly stored our luggage in the back room and gave us claim tickets. Dick had discovered this little gem of advice from the Rick Steves travel guides. We walked across the multiple moats to the Kronborg Castle. From there we had a first view across the water of Sweden. The Kronborg Castle was amazing, completed in 1588, and the place where Shakespeare's Hamlet took place. Very interesting rooms with paintings on the walls and ceiling or panels of paintings affixed to the ceiling. One especially disturbing picture on the ceiling of the King's apartment was of an old man biting onto the stomach of a child. When Dick asked the guide, she said it was about a man that wanted to be immortal and thought that if he ate a child, he would be young again. But the old man was fooled because the child had been fed stones, so he actually died earlier than if he hadn't done it. Ew! The rooms were majestic, but the spiral staircases and stone steps were very treacherous.

Shakespeare

First view of Sweden

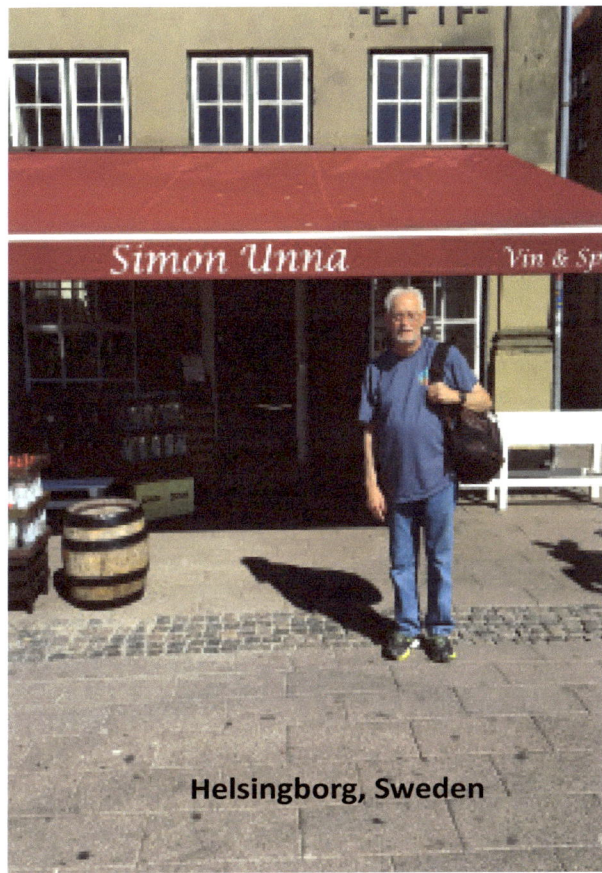

Simon Unna   Vin & Sp

Helsingborg, Sweden

After collecting our luggage at the 7/11, we took the ferry across the North Sea to Helsingbörg, Sweden. I fell in love with Helsingbörg, with its quaint little narrow cobblestone streets and colorful little houses, right up next to each other like townhouses. We stopped at a coffee shop and had croissants and coffee (Dick) and juice (me). I took Dick's picture under an awning from a wine store called Simon. Of all the cities/towns on the trip, this was my favorite. It had kind of an old Scandinavian Key West feel.

We took the bus which cost 120 Swedish krona (SEK) ($13.75 US) each to the Helsingörg airport where Dick had a rental car reserved. Dick caught his foot on an uneven piece of pavement and fell while waiting for the bus and cut his knee and scraped his arm, but no real harm done. The bus went through some interesting little Swedish towns on the way to the airport. In all the ride took approx. 45 minutes. It was a tiny airport, but the car was ready for us. We got a VW Golf with a clip-on Navigation system. Dick could not figure out how to start the car without a pushbutton. We had to ask a lady getting into her car next to us. Her answer, "With the key". Hahaha.

First stop in Sweden was Hasslöv, Halland County, Laholm Municipality. Easy to find the town and churches as the land is very much like eastern Ohio or western Pennsylvania. Lush green rolling hills of mainly farms. We found the Hasslöv church only because it was the only one (no names on any of the churches). Dick found a marker by the church and took a picture. My friend, Lisa Lundin, from Stockholm interpreted it for us, both actual translation, and her interpretation in modern day Swedish.

Church marker in cemetery

The Cemetery (Actual)	The Cemetery Lisa's translation:
is the resting place for the dead	is the resting place of the dead
a room of memories	a place of memories
of God's field	a God's haven
The holy sacred graves	Holy sacred tender hands
Cautious hands	in loving care and
care for nursing and	decorating
decorating	
	The silence on this holy ground
Silence is on this holy ground	
	Teach us how to
Teach us to remember our	honour our days in order to receive
days inorder for us to protect	our wisdom in our hearts
our hearts	

We hunted around the graveyard looking for Hammar and Johnson markers. A young lady stopped to work on her family plot and she spoke English very well. She told us the pastor did not live in town, but the groundskeeper did. However, he was not available at that time. I tried the door of the church, but it was locked so we could not get inside.

It was starting to get late, so we thought we'd better start looking for someplace to spend the night The girl at the cemetery gave us direction to her boyfriend's mother's Bed and Breakfast, but after trying to follow her directions and stopping to ask directions several times, we gave up. We ended up in a little larger town called Laholm and stopped at the hotel. They did not have any vacancies, but we decided to eat dinner at the hotel Pub before moving on.

After calling many places and having a hard time getting through with international calling on our cell phones, we got directions to a small place called Pensionat Enehall. (Pensions are small family run motels similar to B&B but usually larger with multiple rooms. It was very hard to find but we finally got there. A cute little place with separate little buildings with only a few rooms in each building. All painted red. Our room was nice, ground floor with French doors to a little patio. It was definitely in the country because in the morning we could smell the cows. The notes in the guest book advertised a hot tub, clothing optional. We passed on that.

NOTE: We discovered that the reason everyone in Sweden spoke English was because the children are taught English beginning at the age of eleven.

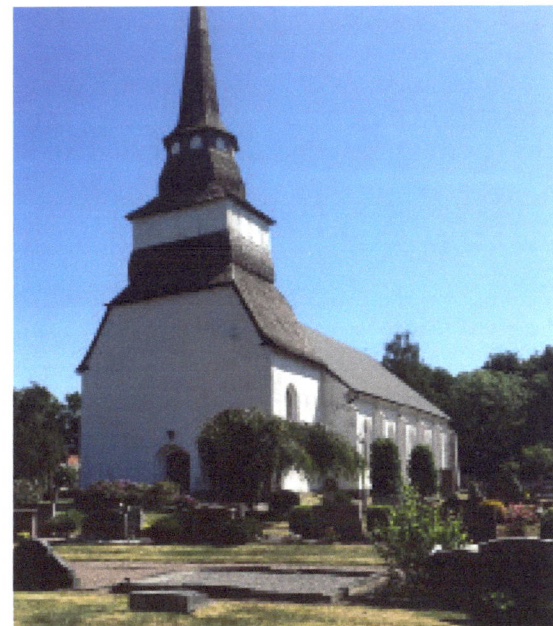

Hasslov Church, Sweden

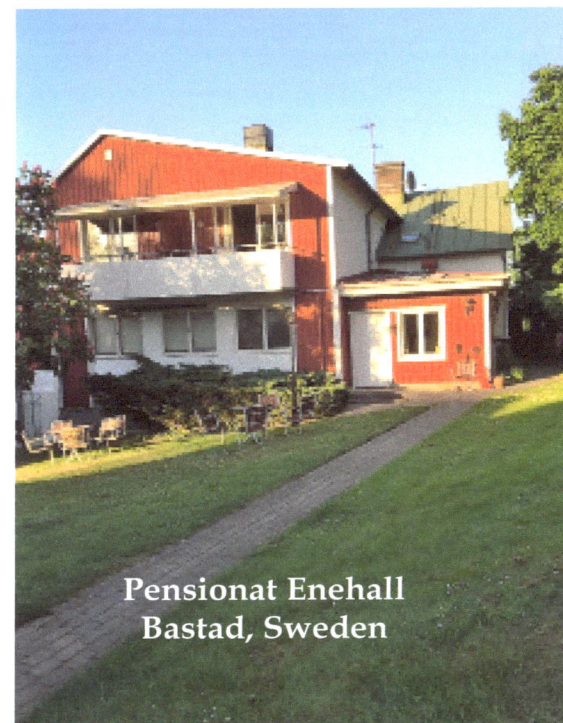

Pensionat Enehall
Bastad, Sweden

Thursday May 24, 2018

Breakfast at the Pensionat Enehell was the best we had had so far. Again, smorgasbord of typical Scandinavian breakfasts, but also scrambled eggs, bacon, croissants, and fresh pickled herring. Dick loved the pickled herring because it was very fresh and went back for seconds.

Båstad, Sweden

We headed into the town of Båstad where we easily found another church, again by looking for the steeple. Dick found a groundskeeper that took us over to the caretaker. He was not very friendly and guarded his information very tightly. We asked about Hammar and Johnson graves but without exact death dates and exact names, he could not help us. We walked around the cemetery looking at tombstones and taking photos. We found several Hammar gravestones but not sure if they were relatives. I tried the door to the church and it was open, so I went in. The organist was practicing and singing *How Great Though Art* in English. I recorded it as I walked through the church. Very beautiful. Every church we went in had these huge beautiful pipe organs. We had heard that the country does not practice much religion, but every church we went to was definitely still be used with services every week. I was glad to see that.

Next to the church was a Visitor Information center. I bought a Swedish coffee cup. I saw a body of water down the small road and asked Dick to drive down to it. The map says the body of water is called Laholmsbukten. But we really could not get very close to the water to find any cute places to stop. Trying to find our way out, we stopped a lady who was walking alongside the road for directions back out to the main road. She asked where we were coming from. I'm sure she meant, what direction, but without thinking, I answered "America." Hahaha — couldn't help me there.

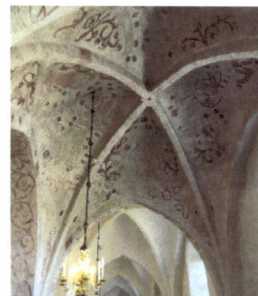

original baptismal font

Bastad Church in Sweden

Enslov, Sweden

After making it back to the main road, we drove to Enslöv, the seat of Enslöv Municipality, Skåne County, Sweden. Dick had some records we could track. Again, very easy to find the church, just look for the steeple. This groundkeeper here was very friendly, and he said that he liked having a chance to practice his English. He solicited the help of another gentlemen but again, without any specific death dates and exact names, could not help much. We walked around this cemetery awhile, saw lots of Johonson, but not Johnson. (Turns out Johnson is Americanized and not used in Sweden)

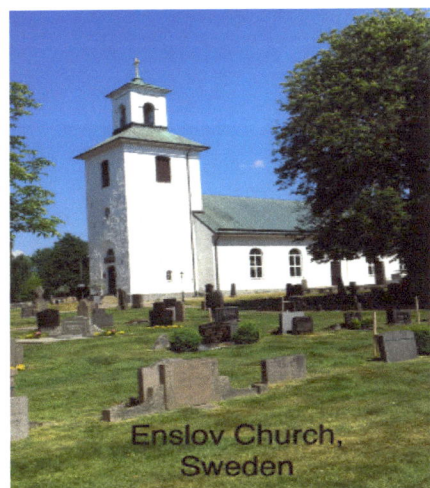

Enslov Church, Sweden

Church at Enslov

Eldsberga, Sweden

We decided to continue on to Eldsberga, Halland County, Halmstad Municipality, Sweden with 720 inhabitants in 2010, according to Wikipedia. I had more specific information about our great-great grandmother *(on Grandpa George Hammar's side)* Johanna Charlotta Svenssen (Jon Svenssen's wife) who died Jan 23, 1908 in Eldsberga. Here, we noticed that like the other cemeteries, there were large grassy areas, up close to the old churches which most assuredly there would have had tombstones at one time. The caretaker explained that in Sweden, gravesites are leased for 25 years. If no one pays to renew the lease, the gravesite is excavated, the remains cremated and ashes spread in their Memory Garden. The stones are broken up to make the stone walls around the cemetery. That way new bodies can be buried in those spots. We were both shocked by this revelation and explained that in America, gravesites are owned, not leased and are never recycled. (I guess since we are a young nation, we still have space to do that – who knows what will happen when the USA is as old as Sweden or Europe. A

friend asked me what happened to the personal effects such as jewelry. Good question. I did not have an answer.

We did not find Johanna Charlotta Svenssen's grave. Perhaps it was recycled. The church was open and we were able to walk through it. The etchings on the walls of these churches are very interesting, rather primitive, drawings instead of painting. But the ceilings are beautiful and ornate. We found a large plot that had once had a fence around it that had all Hammar names on them. We had no idea if these are old relatives or not and questioned why they had not been destroyed. The caretaker, Dennis Selenstrom, said that it was possible that the church made an exception on certain stones and decided to maintain them as part of the church's history. He tried to check his records but his computer was not working. I gave him my email and he promised to email me if he found anything. He emailed me back on June 24 and said that he did not find Johanna Charlotta but that he did find Ana Charlotta 2/20/1786 – 01/12/1845 and twelve other graves and gave us the dates of the records.

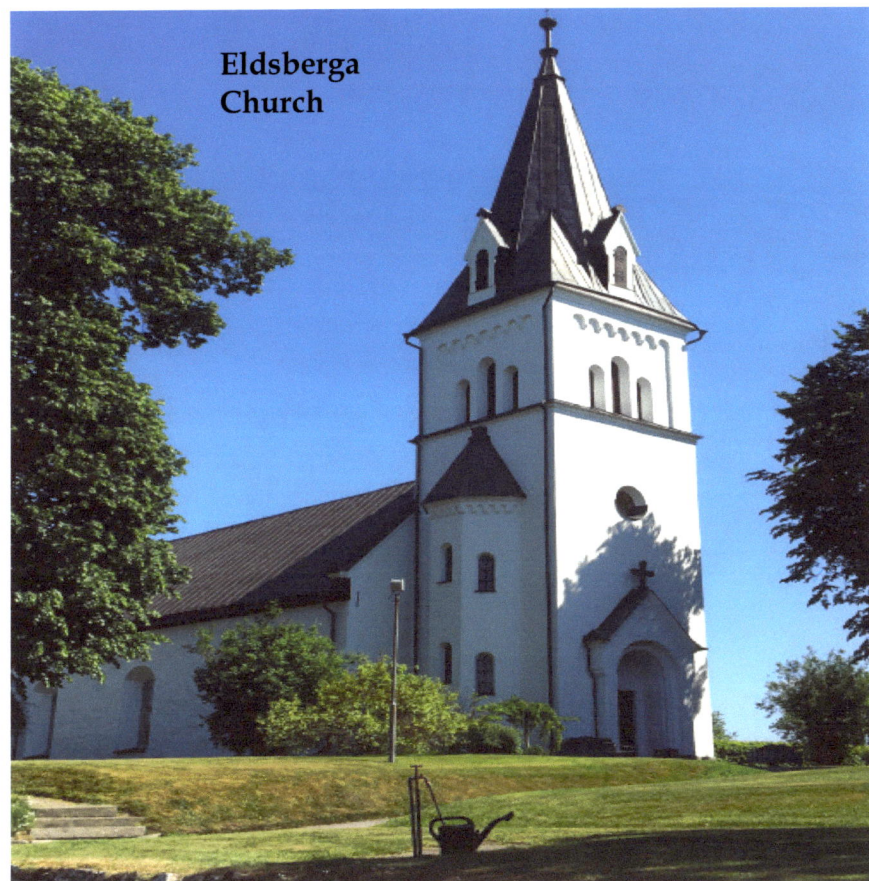

Eldsberga Church

Carl Magnus Hammar
7/25/1819 - 3/6/1887

Louise Frederique Hammar (Ouise)
6/24/1875 - 1/10/1962

Ulla L. Hammar
10/09/1822- 06/10/1852

Carl George Hammar 1859-1860

Louise Hammar
1/20/1847 – 4/15/1864

A.J. Hammar
09/16/1776 - 05/02/1856

B.C. Hammar
09/16/1776 - 05/02/1856

Frederique Hamma
06/27/1849 - 05/15/1868

Hedvig Hammar
10/15/w1832 - 06/16/1909

Hilda Marie Hammar *
07/21/1869 - 07/08/1889

Sophia Hammar
1817-1834

Anders Hammar
1845-1847

Ulla Hammar
1806-1824

Unreadable -Could be Ana Charlotta Hammar
02/20/1786 - 01/12/1845

Eldsberga Hammar plot

Verified by Dennis Selenstrom at svenskakyrken

(Eldesberga Cemetery)

Carl Magnus Hammar 7/25/1819 - 3/6/1887

Louise Frederique Hammar 6/24/1875 - 1/10/1962 (stone says Ouise)

Ulla L. Hammar 10/09/1822- 06/10/1852

Louise Hammar 1/20/1847 – 4/15/1864 (stone looks like Souise)

Carl Georg Hammar 1859 - 1860

A.J. Hammar 9/16/1776 - 5/02/1856

B.C. Hammar 9/16/1776 -5/02/1856

Fredrique Hammar 6/27/1849 - 5/15/1868

Hedvig Hammar 10/15/1832 - 4/16/1909

Hilda de Mare Hammar 7/21/1869 - 7/8/1889 (*not on Dennis list)

Sofia Hammar 1817 - 1834 (looks like Sofie on stone)

Anders Hammar 1845 – 1847

Ulla Hammar 1806-1824

Carl Magnusta Hammar 07/25/1819 – 03/06/1887

   (not found by Dick)

Unknown Hammar – could be Ana Charlotta Hammar

 Ana Charlotta Hammar 02/20/1786 – 01/12/1845

   (not found by Dick)

To live in the hearts of others is never to die.

#Rest in Peace

Hammar plot in Eldsberga

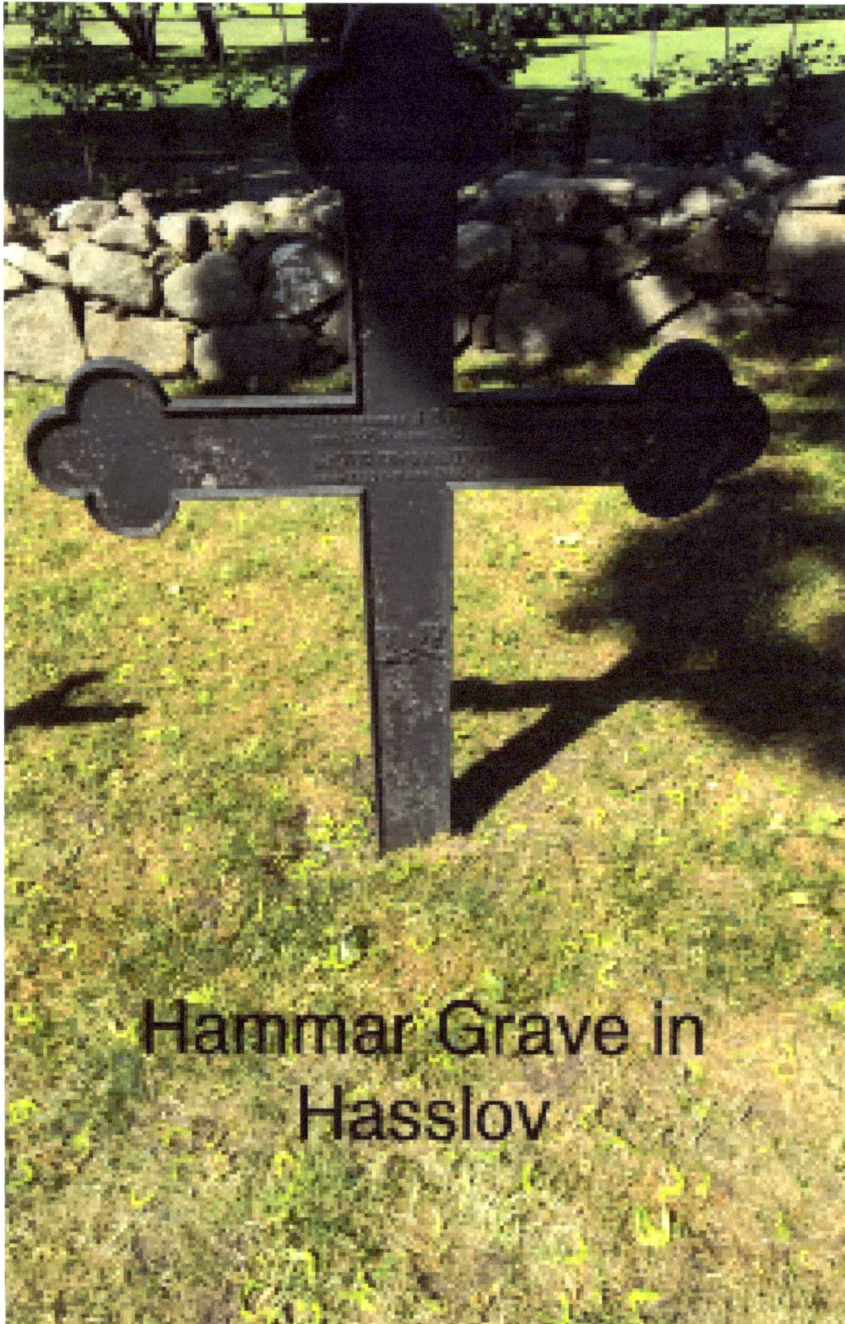

Hammar Grave in Hasslov

Hasslov, Sweden

On a whim, we decided to go back to the Hasslöv and look around the cemetery again. (I don't remember why) This time Dick found an iron cross with the name J.E. Hammar on it along the perimeter of the grave yard with several other crosses.

We took a picture of it and sent it to Gene who agreed this was our 5th great-grand-father on our mother's side because it even had his wife's name, Hedwig Charlotta Wesstrom on it. This was an exciting find. Gene verified what it said.

J.E. Hammar 1779-1845

Hedwig Charlotta Wesstrom 1795-1866

We wondered if there was a significance to the iron crosses all being together, like perhaps it meant they were military or something. A caretaker at another cemetery said no, there was no significance since Sweden hadn't been in a war for two hundred years. He did say that making crosses out of iron was a lower cost alternative at the time for those that could not afford an engraved stone. On later thought, I reasoned those crosses were in a row because they were from excavated graves and put against the stone wall along the border of the graveyard together because they did not deteriorate like the stone gravestones. So, I believe J.E. Hammar's grave was not in that spot but the cross was set near the wall later. A lucky find for us. But who knows for sure?

Gothenburg,Sweden

We left the area and headed to Gothenburg to spend the night where we had a reservation. It is the second largest city in Sweden. Interesting fact per Wikipedia; "The region on the west coast of Sweden has been inhabited for several thousands of years. During the Stone Age, there was incidentally a settlement right on present day Gothenburg." The city of Gothenburg is not pretty at all, a big busy, old city, built in 1621. Every street and highway seemed to be under construction and our GPS could not keep up with the highway changes. We ended up driving around and around in circles, continually missing the correct turns because I couldn't tell Dick fast enough as the GPS directions kept changing. When we finally found Hotel Huttl it was not in a very nice part of town. We would have cancelled but found out that the room was non-refundable since it was booked on Booking.com. They didn't have any parking near-by except on the street and no spots close. They did have a parking garage a few blocks over, so we opted to use the parking garage and walk.

The one good thing about the hotel was the front desk girls were really very friendly once we settled into the idea of staying there. We started telling them about why

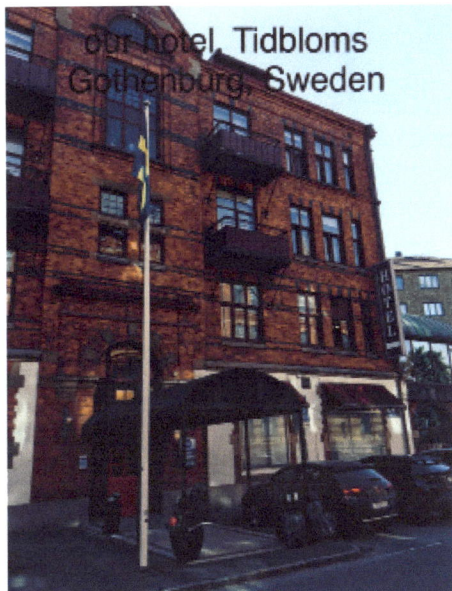
our hotel, Tidbloms Gothenburg, Sweden

we were in Sweden and our ancestral roots. On a whim, I told them about the Swedish prayer we had always said when we were children. I had been told that it was all gibberish, but they said, other than some wrong pronunciations, which is not surprising considering we were children and had only repeated what we thought we heard, we weren't too far off.

The way I always said it was, "

Shera Gud, Vas ingin mutton, Yes um, Um Uman."

She gave us the actual interpretation which is:

"Dear God, Bless the food, In Jesus Name, Amen."

In Swedish, the correct spelling and pronunciation is (per our desk clerk):

"Kära gud, Välsigna maten i jesus namn, Amen"

I was glad to know that what I had been saying was not gibberish, even though I believe God would have understood anyhow.

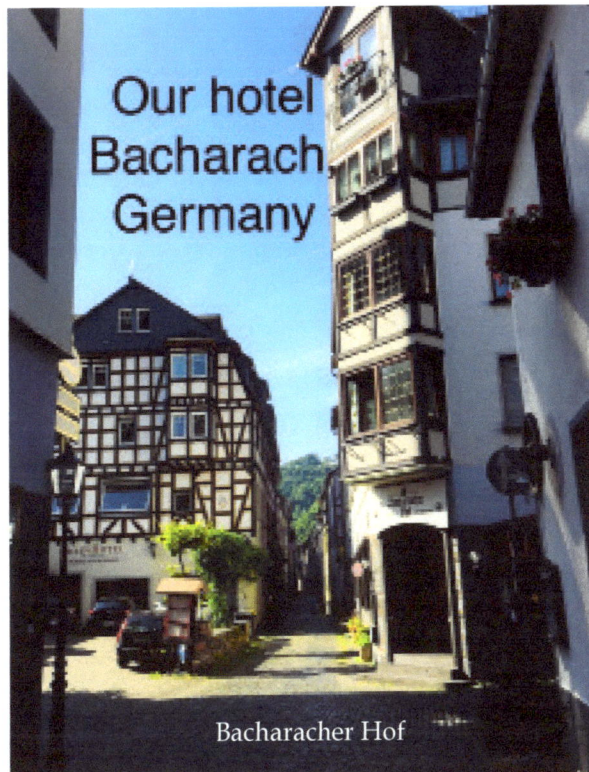
Our hotel Bacharach, Germany

Bacharacher Hof

Friday May 25, 2018 –

Bacharach, Germany

Extremely surprising, the breakfast at this hotel was the best we had had on our entire trip. Lots of fresh fruit, bacon, eggs, croissants, other pastries, juice. All very fresh and very, very good. Except for the moving sesame seeds, *ants* on the sweets!

We left Gothenburg (my least favorite city) and drove to the airport. Turned in our car and took SAS airlines first to Stockholm, then on to Frankfurt.

SAS lost our luggage in Frankfurt but promised it would be on the next plane coming in at 7:30 p.m. We decided to stick around the airport until our luggage showed up, have dinner and then head to the hotel. Dick and I did not agree on what to eat at the Food Court, so I had McDonald's and he had Thai food. Customer service at the lost luggage desk explained how we would have to come back to baggage claim through a door that had a doorbell beside it. We questioned about going back through customs. The guy just laughed and said not to worry about it. Sure enough, we walked right through with no one even checking anything. Finding the mystery door to get back to baggage claim without going back through security proved to be challenging. Every door looked alike and none like the picture they gave us. Almost by accident we finally found the door with the doorbell and they let us in. The same customer service clerk came from around his desk, laughing, and asked us what we thought of their customs? A guy in a uniform walked by and he said, "There goes our Customs Agent now, going to lunch." As it turns out, there are no customs checks when traveling from one European country to another, but we did not know that.

We collected our luggage. Next feat was finding our rental car. We had already checked in at the Budget/Avis desk and got the keys, but finding the car was another subject. Even with the help of two guys, neither of which spoke English, we finally found our car in the garage which was two levels down. This car was a black Opel SUV. Again, with stick shift.

Car loaded, we headed out of Frankfurt west to Bacharach, Germany, along the Rhein River. We had reservations at the Bacharacher Hof hotel. We got there quite late, but they were waiting for us. The family lives in the building. Our room was ready for us and the hotel owner spoke English pretty well. The room was small but accommodating and clean. Bacharach is a very interesting little old German town.

We had to pass under a big stone archway to enter the town which dated back to 1322.

We found that the hotels and restaurants usually had English speaking people, but if you stopped a stranger on the streets of Germany to ask directions they rarely chose to speak English even though they might know some. I would approach and ask, "English?" and usually get a gruff "No." They obviously are not taught English in school like the Swedes. A little history of Bacharach, *per a brochure of the city*, it was founded by the Celts and later passed into possession of the Archbishop of Cologne. All this took place before 1194 when it passed into the hands of the Wells

of Brunswick. I could not find the actual date of when the town was founded. The brochure said the Protestant church was started in 1100. In the Middle Ages, Bacharach was the main trading center for wines for the middle Rhein. The grape arbors can be seen by boat as a backdrop above Bacharach. One of the most interesting cities we visited.

Saturday, May 26, 2018 -

After a lovely breakfast at the hotel, we decided to take a ferry boat ride down the Rhein from Bacharach to Boppard, the most scenic sections of the Rhein. We decided to drive up to Boppard and take the ferry back down to Bacharach, then later take the train back up to the car. Easy enough in theory. The ferry boat had two levels with both outside and inside seating. We found seating in the front of the second level outside where we could get the best view, including the view of the man in the leather Lederhosen. We saw lots of castles sitting high on the hills above grape arbors and the charming small towns along the river. Most impressive were the many ornate churches. It was a slow, beautiful ride. We were fortunate not to have any rain for the entire trip. A few times, we experienced rain drops while we were driving, but whenever we reached our destinations, the sun came back out.

We left our car by the river at Bacharach in anticipation of an easy trip back via train from Boppard. After having access to a car most of the trip, waiting on trains was not pleasant but we told ourselves we were in no hurry. Things went wrong when we got off the train at the wrong Bacharach stop, not realizing that there were two. After much confusion hunting for our car and not seeing anything familiar, we realized that we had to get back on the train and go one more stop. Ah, there was the car, right where we left it. What we planned as a half day outing turned into almost a full day.

Back in the car, we drove to the Moselle Valley and checked in to Hotel Traube, built in 1852 right along the Moselle River in the town of Löf, Germany. Traube means "grape" according to their brochure. We didn't have reservations, but the owner said he had a room for us. Dick asked to see it, explaining that we wanted two single beds. He gave us keys but the beds were joined together with

Rhein River Cruise

a single headboard. We went back down and Dick explained to the man who did not speak much English that we preferred a different room, He pointed to me and said, "This is my sister!" Ahhh. The expression when it dawned on him was quite comical. This room was nice and had space between the beds.

Dinner at the hotel was a little tense as they did not have an English menu and the waitress was not at all helpful in wanting to explain things in English. Luckily two young men at the next table spoke English so one helped us with the menu. (I think he said that he was from Minnesota and he was a student in Germany for a year). He also told us about how to get to the Eltz Castle that we planned to visit on Sunday. After walking around town, and not finding any place for a cocktail, we settled back at the hotel for drinks on the outside patio. The same waitress was much nicer this time when we tried to tip her for our drinks and almost gave her way too much and she was nice enough to tell us it was too much.

(Stupid Americans)

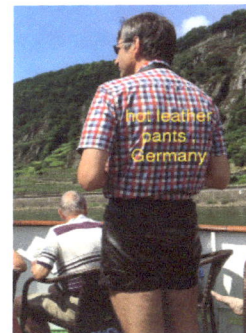

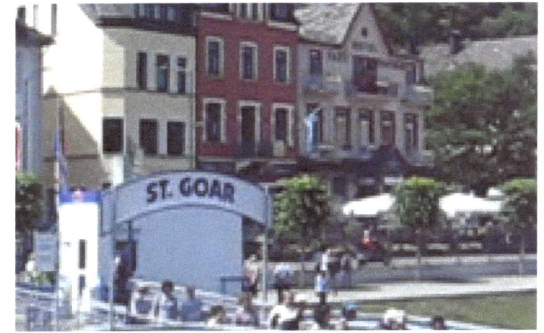

Sunday May 27, 2018

We followed the GPS and took a very winding road to get to the castle and discovered after we reached the top that there was a much more direct route on a highway. In the parking lot, we had the choice of walking to the castle or taking the shuttle. We opted for the shuttle and I'm glad we did (round trip for 2 Euros each- $2.35 US). The way up was very steep. I never would have made it. Eltz Castle is amazing with many of the rooms with authentic furnishings. We took the guided tour and glad we did. According to the brochure and the guide, the Eltz family built the first structure nearly 1000 years ago. The Eltz family controlled the trade along the Moselle River in medieval days. Over time, three branches of the Eltz family built homes on the castle complex, one in 1472 and two others in 1540. This section of the castle complex was the one built in 1472. Despite many wars over the centuries, the castle stayed intact because the Eltz family always sided with whoever was most in power at the time. The castle's Great Hall was amazing, A fool's mask indicated that free speech was permitted by everyone inside. A rose (the symbol of silence) meant that nothing said while in council could be repeated beyond the door. The Armory and Treasury had case after case, room after room of weapons and china, tapestries, gold and silver belongings of the Eltz family. Photography was not allowed inside the castle so we could not photo any of it.

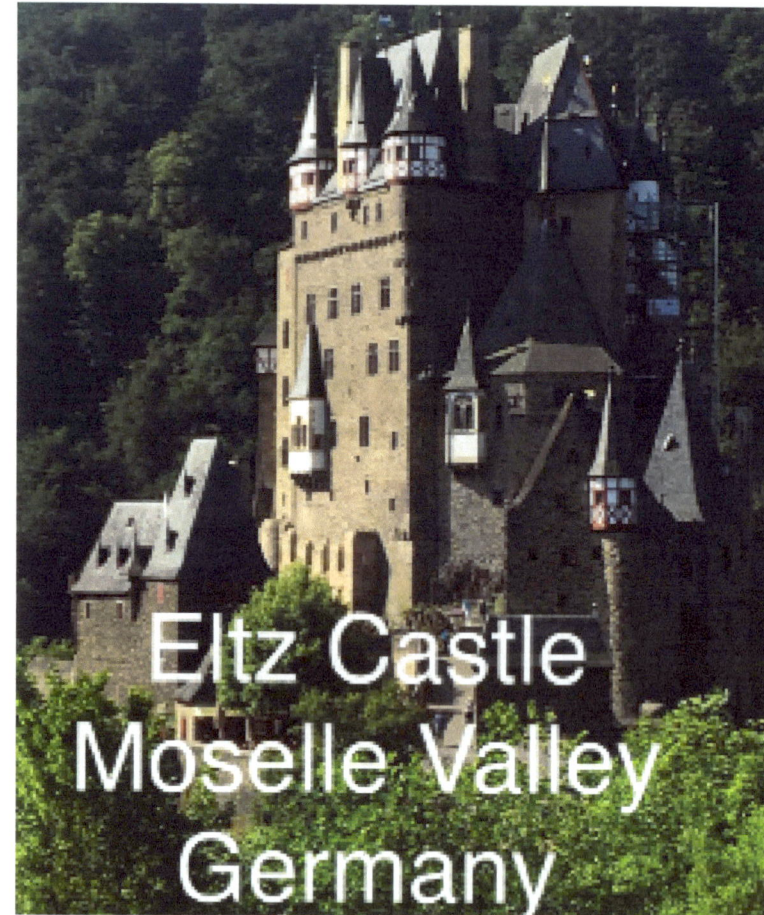

Eltz Castle
Moselle Valley
Germany

Birkenfeld, Gemany

We left the Moselle valley and drove to Birkenfeld, Germany where I thought we could find the roots of our Simon ancestors, our immigrant ancestor, Great-great-great-great grandfather John Adam Simon. Born in April 26, 1716 and baptized in the Evangelisch, Kirchberg (Evangelical Church of Rheinland) on August 23, 1716. We found the church, but it wasn't open. Someone told us that the Birkenfeld Museum was open so we walked over to it. The gentleman and his wife spent a lot of time talking to us and showed us the original stones from the first protestant church before being replaced by the current one on the same grounds in 1885, . He had a lot of history about Birkenfeld, including artifacts from Roman times. I was awestruck to think that we were walking on our real ancestral roots of the town. (note: Gene has since disputed this and said he thought we were in the wrong town – very disappointing. We should have been in Suzlbach-Birkenfeld, about 38 miles away or Herren-Sulzbach, about 25 miles. My feeling about that: – I bet John Adam still walked those same grounds – the towns were very close together. I'm going to count it) Just as we were about to leave, I noticed the church doors were open so Dick parked the car and we went in. Two young girls were practicing singing (in English) *I Have Loved You for a Thousand Years.* It brought tears to my eyes. I took a video while they were singing and some pictures of the inscriptions on the walls.

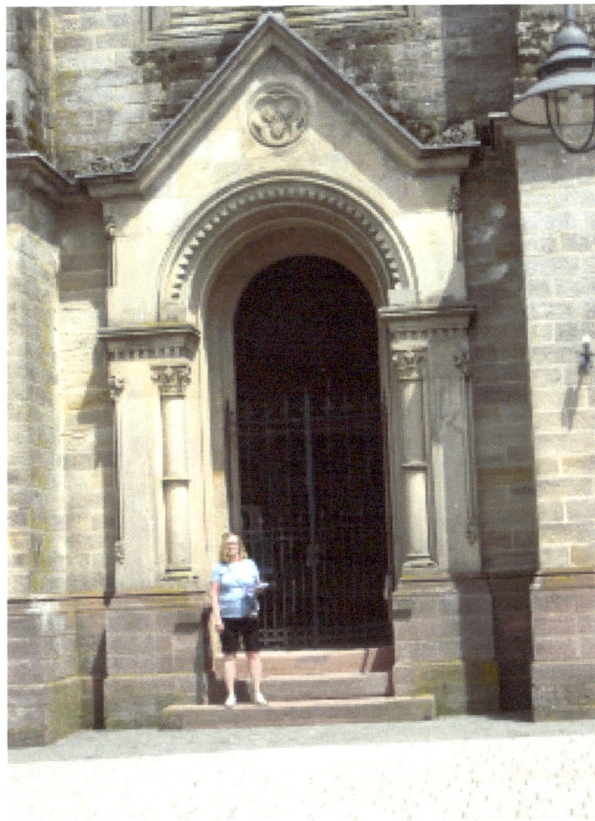

Beware of the Devil tempting the sheep

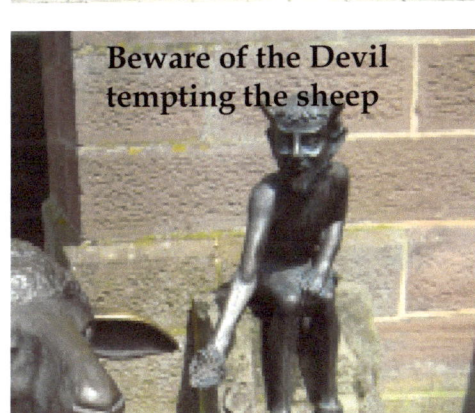

hotel in Worms,

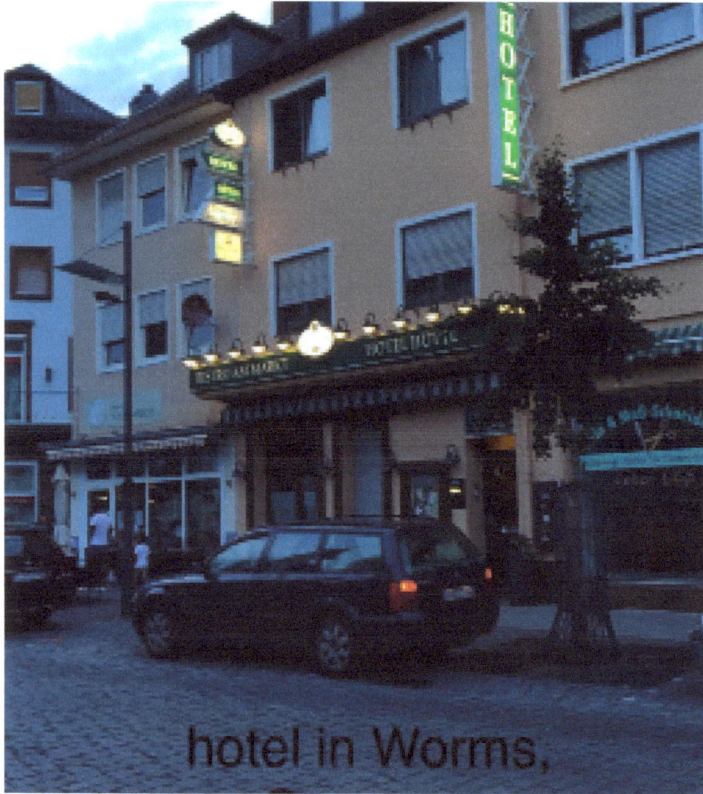

Leaving Birkenfeld, we drove to Worms, Germany, claimed to be the oldest city in Germany, founded over a 1000 years ago and with artifacts dating back 6000 years. This is a darling little town, lots of churches. We spent quite a bit of time walking around the town. There is a wonderful monument to Martin Luther, where here, he began the Protestant Reformation away from the Catholic Church.

We checked into Hotel Huttl in Worms for the night. The hotel had very steep steps getting up to the main floor and it was hard to get our luggage up. The hotel clerk said it was okay to park across the street, but a policeman came by yelling at Dick in German to move, so he had to park a little bit away. This was the only place that we took two separate rooms since it was so affordable. ($58.67 US) The rooms were small, but very clean. I had the best meal of the whole trip at a small restaurant close to the hotel; goulash with roasted potatoes. To die for! We had a nice Chardonnay and ice cream sundaes for dessert. We walked around town some more and went back to the same restaurant and sat on their outside back patio for one more cocktail. We discovered that nothing is open on Sunday here, not any stores, most restaurants, no bars, nothing.

Dick was getting messages from Steve that his little dog, Willis, was not doing well. He would not eat and his insulin levels were askew. I think he was having separation anxiety being away from Dick.

The Luther Monument (Lther-Denkmal) in Worms is the largest Reformation monument in the world and contains nine statues and eight portrait medallions of the most important figures in the Protestant Reformation.   (*Worms website*)
The international memorial to the Reformation, 1868. Luther's hymn, Ein feste Burg ist under Gott / A Mighty Fortress is our God" is transfomred here into stone. (*Fotoeins on May 15, 2017*) One my personal favorite hymns
It was getting dark by the time we got to the statue so it was too dark to capture all the reformers surrounding Martin Luther.

Christoph Kern

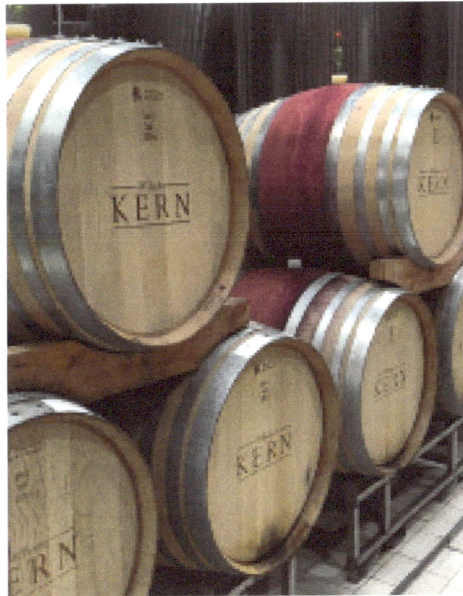

Kern Winery

Wilhelm - Maybach, Germany

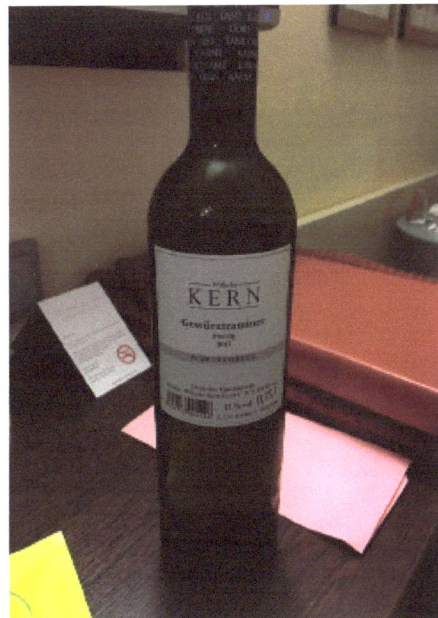

Monday May 28, 2018

After breakfast at the hotel, we headed toward Munich. We had to take a detour off the Autobahn to get gas (no gas stations on there) and stopped in Stuttgart for lunch (our new normal – dessert and a drink) We had the best desserts ever outside on a picnic table from a little store with two very pleasant older ladies that spoke almost no English.

That scrumpuous dessert? After sending this picture to Todd Space for translation, instead of getting the coveted name, I learned that it said, "assorted breakfast pastries." That was no help at all. But Amy's friend, Laurence's husband is a master Chef. Chef Emery said it was made with Hefeteig dough, filled with vanilla cream and topped with fresh strawberries and glaze. Yum!

At a second stop, we inquired about local wineries. Then we programmed the GPS for a winery from the recommendations of the shopkeeper.

We found the Kern Winery in Wilhelm-Maybach, more by accident than by the GPS, which got us close but not exactly to it. One of the owners, Christoph Kern, a 5th generation Kern owner gave us a private tour, even though they don't usually give tours without a large group. He was very nice and taught a lot about wine making. He took us through all the steps from when the grapes first arrive in the truck to bottled and ready for sale. After the tour, we did some wine sampling and bought a bottle, Grauburgunder, a Pinto Grigio for us to drink back at the hotel. Great price, only $7.80 US. Wonderful wine.

In Munich, we checked into the Hotel Leonardo, where we had reservations. By far, the most upscale hotel and our room had two queen beds, a first on our trip, a refrigerator, safe and desk. We will be here three days so it is nice to have a little more room.

Dick made plans with Susan, Corrie's cousin, that lives in Rosenheim. She would meet up with us on Tuesday. Susan speaks German so that helps.

Tuesday, May 29, 2018

Dachau, Germany

We had breakfast at the hotel (first time not included in the price) and drove to Dachau City, site of the Nazi Dachau Concentration camp. We were given hand held speakers, set to English. We only had to select the corresponding number to the item we were looking at to get the history behind it, i.e.: the barracks, main grounds for inspections and roll call, the gas chambers, ovens, etc. Most of the barracks were gone but there were two that had been rebuilt to replicate the barracks at the time. Very primitive. Rows and rows of wood bunks connected together, three high. One thing they said was each day inspection was done, the stripes on the thin blankets over the straw mattresses had to be perfectly lined up or the inmates would be punished. They were not allowed to lay on the bunks during the day unless they were very sick or dying. Only about three wooden benches and one wooden table was beside the bunks, not enough for all the inmates. If they did not get a seat, they had to stand – not allowed to sit on the floor or their beds. Just another form of torture. Unbelievable to imagine such a thing.

The most hair-raising thing for me was to stand in the gas chamber. Four rooms joined together, the 1st, where they stripped and were told to go into the "showers". The "showers" were the gas chamber. The next room was the ovens (only two there and one more in another building) and the last room is where the bodies were stacked to the ceiling until they could get to them to be burned. I was surprised at how small the ovens were, not much wider than a normal 30" kitchen oven, but deeper to hold the height of the bodies. I am glad that I went, but I have no desire to ever go back to any other camps. I get it, I understand. I don't want to see anymore.

NOTE: It was interesting to learn that Dachau and other concentration camps where used right after the war ended to house displaced people who had no place to stay because of the bombing. The barracks and many of the buildings in the camps where rebuilt by the Americans to help with the relief effort which is why the original camp structures only exists in photographs.

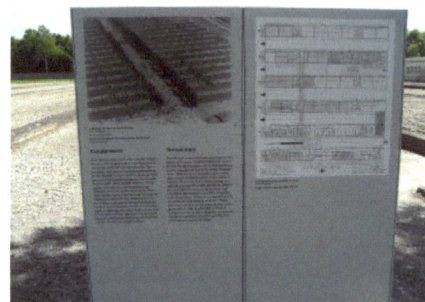

the ovens

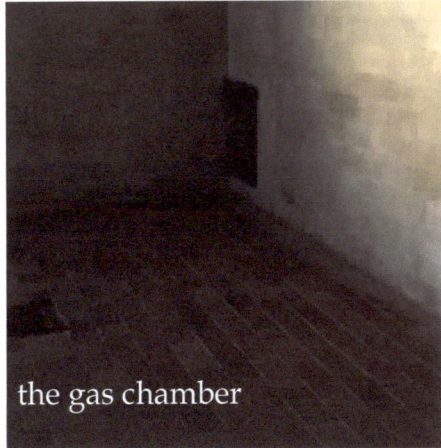

the gas chamber

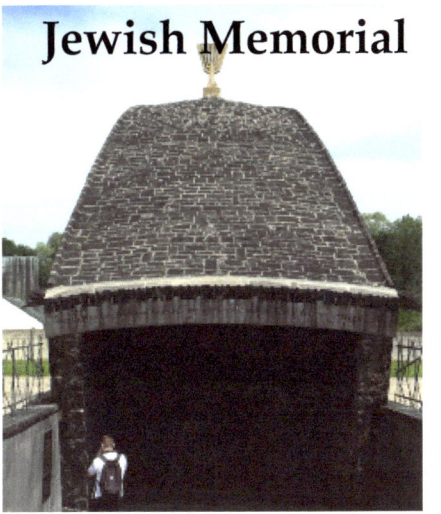

Jewish Memorial

MAHNMAL
ZUM GEDENKEN
AN DIE JÜDISCHEN MÄRTYRER,
DIE IN DEN JAHREN 1933 - 1945
NATIONALSOZIALISTISCHER
SCHRECKENSHERRSCHAFT
UMGEKOMMEN SIND.
IHR TOD BEDEUTET UNS
MAHNUNG UND VERPFLICHTUNG

ERRICHTET VOM LANDESVERBAND
DER ISRAELITISCHEN KULTUS =
GEMEINDEN IN BAYERN IM JAHRE
1967 / 5727

Dachau Concentration Camp

foundations
of
barracks

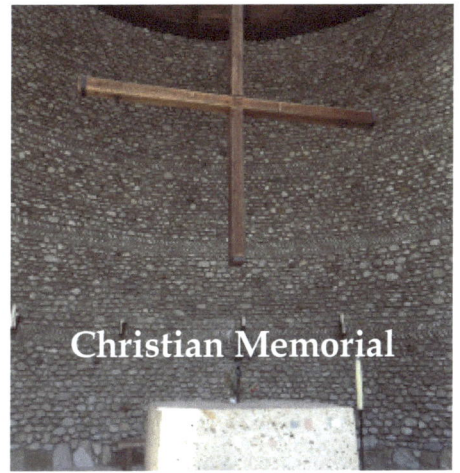

Christian Memorial

Rosenheim, Germany

We drove to Rosenheim and met up with Susan (Corrie's cousin) at the ferry terminal going to the Herrenchiemsee Island, where King Ludwig II's Summer Palace is. A pleasant change from Dachau. The autoban was interesting. Dick was going about 120 kph (75 mph) but people were passing us like we were standing still. He kept trying to get me to take a picture of this church with the Alps in the background. He'd say, "Now, take it now!" Of course going that fast, this was a near impossible feat. It wan't until I got home that I discovered that I did get the shot. (Cover photo)

Susan was nice enough to have already purchased our tickets for the ferry. It was a fifteen-minute walk after getting off the ferry to the palace, going through meadows and gardens with several large fountains. The palace itself is magnetically furnished from 1878 when the castle was begun. It was never finished before his death. I have never seen anything so opulent in all my life. So over the top it wasn't even pretty. He had to have been the most egotistical, jack-ass that ever lived. Four huge rooms were built strictly to show off with no intention of ever using them, including a the State bedchamber to the right. Ludwig was obsessed with the castle in Versailles and built this as a replica, except larger and more ornate. The grand hall had at least six huge chandeliers that held over a 100 candles each plus huge sconces on the walls with another 50 or so candles. He only lived in the castle for ten days before a mysterious death that still has not been solved. He made his servants light all the candles in all the rooms every night just so he could walk through them. (If I was them, I would have killed him myself – maybe they did.) This is the same Ludwig II that built the Neuschwanstein Castle that Walt Disney fashioned the Castle in Disney after. We did not go to that one because it was such a long distance away and Susan said this one was more decorated and actually more interesting.

Susan did not stay with us during the tour since she had done it several times. After coming back on the ferry, Dick and I had dinner at a restaurant close to the ferry. We ate outside under a sun umbrella while enjoying the pure German atmosphere of architecture around us, complete with window boxes filled with geraniums.

From texts, Willis still not doing well back home. I know this was weighing on Dick.

photo frorm the brochure

The State Bedchamber in Herrenchiemsee Palace

1st view of the Alps

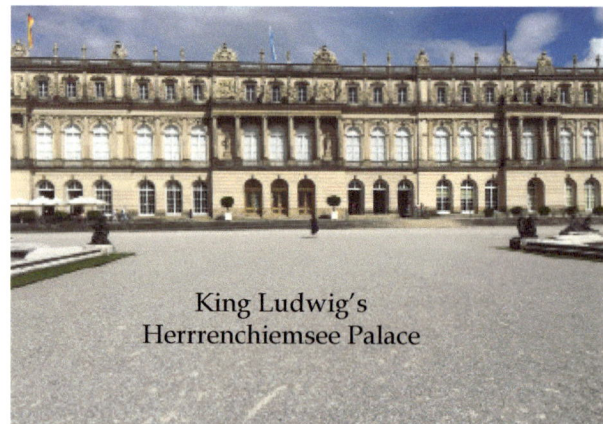

King Ludwig's Herrrenchiemsee Palace

Wednesday, May 30, 2018

Salzburg, Austria

Susan met us at the Rosenheim train station. She had already bought our train tickets. The train ride to Salzburg, Austria took us through areas where we could see the Alps but not really that close to them. The train station in Salzburg was very modern, like a small airport station.

We spoke to a person at the Salzburg station Visitor Center and decided not to go to the meadow where Maria sang *The Hills are Alive* in the Sound of Music because it was a ninety-minute bus ride, then a forty-five minutes hike up the hill. The guide said you had to have on very good walking shoes and Susan and I only had on sandals. I told Dick and Susan that we could find any hill with the Alps in the background for me to pretend I was there. Dick wasn't too excited about doing the Sound of Music tour, but he was a good sport and we bought tickets for the Hop On- Hop Off City bus so we could stop at only the sites that I wanted to see the most.

First, we went to the Mirabellplatz where I jumped down the steps singing, "Doe, a deer, a female deer, Ray, a drop of morning sun . . ." (much to Dick's embarrassment) I flung my arms wide and danced around the Pegasus Fountain in the gardens while Susan took a video. I was in heaven. We took the bus passed Mozart's house where he was born and later lived and would later see it again on foot. Jumping on and off the bus, we went passed the Pferdeschwemme Horse Bath and found our way to the Nonnberg Abbey. We stopped at a little outside café for refreshment. Dick stayed there, while Susan and I climbed the 150 steps to the Abbey. I was surprised to see how small the gate and door to the Abbey really was. I pictured it much larger. That is as far as we could go because it is still an active cloister for nuns. The view up there was amazing looking over Salzburg and across from the Fortress Hohensalzburg, that can be seen looking over Salzburg from almost anywhere.

Back on the bus, we made it to the Sound of Music Pavilion -*not in same location as the movie.* I made Dick join hands with me in a mock pose of Liesel and Rolf. He had no idea what he was doing. Susan took that great camera shot. It was a little bit of bus ride out of town to Palace Leopold where the Von Trapp family lived in the Sound of Music. *Actually, only the exterior shots were taken here.* We got off the bus and walked all around the man-made lake behind the house. We could not get close to it, but it was breathtaking from across the water to see the famed patio. With my fill of Sound of Music, *except for my meadow*, we spent the rest of the day walking around Salzburg and shopping. Susan took us to a section of town where all the shops were. I bought an Austrian Christmas ornament with an Edelweiss on it and some beer glasses for Tai and Todd. Dick bought an apron for Sarah.

We were very tired from all the walking and caught the train back to Rosenheim. Susan took us to an outside beer garden where we had a terrific meal and we finally got to repay her by buying her meal. Such a nice girl. I was determined to have sausage on my last night in Austria/Germany before we headed home. Susan kept wanting to order me something else – nope, I wanted sausage. And they were good. Along with my favorite beer – Carlsberg. Dick had Beef Cheeks and the beer garden's own Flotzinger Brau beer. Susan drinks beer with 7up. She said the locals do that so they can drink more and not get drunk. We said goodbye and Thank You to Susan and headed back to Munich.

Hop On Hop Off Bus in Salszburg

Doe a Deer, a female deer, Ray, s drop of golden sun

Prancing aound the Pegasus Fountain

Mozart's Birth place, Salzburg

The Horse Baths

Gate of Nonnborg Abbey

Fortress Hohensalzburg

Susan and Joanne @ Palace Leopold

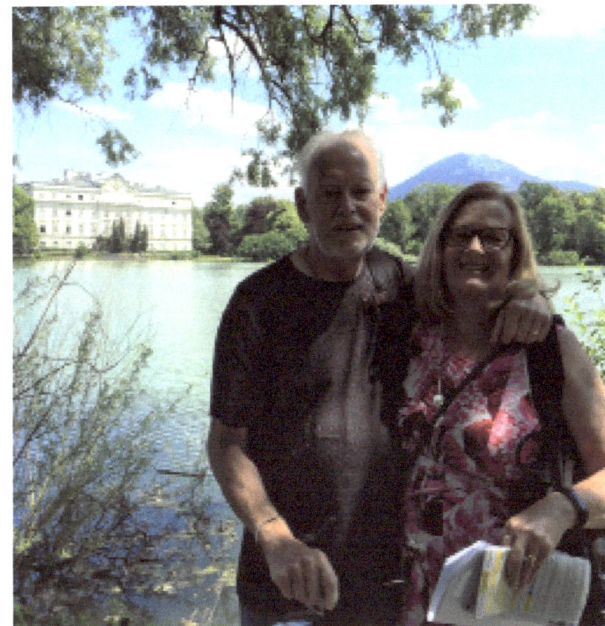

Dick and Joanne @ Palace Leopold

"I am sixteen going on seventeen....."

The Leopold Palace

Thursday, May 31, 2018

Frankfurt - Brussels - Copenhagen - Fort Lauderdale

We woke early and opted not to have breakfast at the hotel, instead getting on the road from Munich to Frankfurt since our flight was at 6:50 a.m. We dropped the car at the Frankfurt airport. First leg home was from Frankfurt to Brussels. Changing planes in Brussels, to Copenhagen, Denmark. We had to collect our checked luggage in Copenhagen and make sure they got on the flight home. Then it was time for the long nine-hour flight back from Copenhagen to Fort Lauderdale, Florida. I don't know what we were thinking, but after hauling around extra jackets the whole trip, we both had packed our jackets. The plane was freezing. I had a scarf I wrapped around myself that helped a little, but Dick did not have much. He finally went into the restroom and added another short sleeve shirt under his long sleeve. It was a long, cold, miserable flight.

Terri picked us up at the Fort Lauderdale airport (with Cooper asleep in the backseat). We were glad to be on US soil.

Friday, June 1, 2018

Miami, Florida

Terri took us on a car ride tour of Miami in the morning, then we went with Todd to several bars and to a brewery where he explained making beer. Interesting. Cooper came along and had fun playing with Gaga (me) the whole time.

Saturday, June 2, 2018

Fort Lauderdale, Florida to Las Vegas, NV or Marco Island, FL

Dick drove my car to the Fort Lauderdale airport (I don't drive on I-95), I dropped him off to head back to Las Vegas, then I took the back roads toward Weston where I picked up I-75 and headed home to Marco Island. I did not realize I was so tired, but with Tai still in Virginia for Keith's high school graduation, I slept for about 24 hours straight.

Thanks for the memories. It was the trip of a lifetime.

Denmark   Sweden   Germany   Austria

Christmas Ornaments from each country

Most of the information we had to begin this adventure was recorded by our mother, Bernice Hammar Simon who spent many years researching our geneology. She put toegether a wonderful book of data and stories about our ancestors that brought them to life. Each of us received a notebook on July 30, 1984. What a keepsake! Many people don't know this, but her interest in geneology began when I came home from high school in 1964 with a project to trace my family tree as far back as I could. Mom never stopped researching after that. She even had a bumper sticker that read "I collect dead relatives." As technology increased, most of her data was transferred to a program called Roots, or Roots3, then to Ultimate Family Tree and our Dad started inputting into Ancestry.com. Ancestry.com (not Dad) wasn't always accurate and that is how we ended up in the wrong towns sometimes. Gene has done the most checking to verify or correct the information on Ancestry.com. There is also FamilySearch.org, which is the Church of the Latter Day Saints website, probably the most accurate of all. We were told that the best Swedish records are archived in Lund, Sweden for our Swedish side, but it is not online and we did not have time to go there. Regardless, we certainly made some discoveries to add to that data.

I also used Wikipedia to get general information about some of the places we visited as well as information from brochures we picked up along the way. I hope this book encourages others to set out and *Chase your Roots......and then some*.

www.ingramcontent.com/pod-product-compliance
Lightning Source LLC
Chambersburg PA
CBHW042106090426

42811CB00018B/1869